Insider Secrets to College Classroom Success!
© 2015 by Antoinette Smith. All rights reserved.

Published by Freedom Stream in the United States of America.

ISBN 13: 978-0-9857304-2-0
ISBN 10: 0-9857304-2-0

All rights reserved. The reproduction, transmission or utilization of this work in whole or in part in any form by any electronic, mechanical or other means, now known or hereafter invented, including xerography, photocopying and recording, or in any information storage or retrieval system, is forbidden
without written permission. For written permission, please contact Freedom Stream, 1421 SW 107th Avenue, Ste. 230, Miami, FL 33174 U.S.A.

Names and identifying characteristics of certain individuals in this book have been changed in order to protect their privacy.

Scripture taken from the NEW AMERICAN STANDARD BIBLE®, Copyright ©1960, 19 62,1963,1968,1971,1972,1973,1975,1977,1995 by The Lockman Foundation. Used by permission.

www.drantoinettesmith.com

Copy Editor: E. Claudette Freeman/E. Claudette Freeman Literary Services
Cover Design: Christoper Thomas of Chris Thomas Graphics
Interior Design: Brandi K. Etheredge

INSIDER SECRETS to College Classroom SUCCESS!

Dr. Antoinette Smith, PhD

Dear student:

My gift to you, with tips and tricks. Enjoy :-)

— Prof. Smith

About the Author

Professor Antoinette Smith earned her PhD in 2004. She is a faculty member of accounting, teaching both graduate and undergraduate students.

She is a faculty member of academia and a faculty member of collegial life; and has the secrets to college classroom success gathered from her personal observation and that of faculty members of Harvard, University of Miami, University of Texas at Austin, Yale, Florida International University, Miami University, and more. Whenever she shares her wisdom about college success, students always respond, "I wish someone told me that information when I entered college." At the suggestion of many of her students, she has penned these successful tips every college student should know.

Table Of Contents

Introduction 7

#1: Know The Faculty Member 11

#2: Establish a Positive Student Profile 17

#3: Learn to Make Tough Decisions 29

#4: Be A Team Player 39

#5: Prepare for the Unexpected 43

Bonus Advice - Beyond the Classroom 51

Acknowledgements

To my college students, thank you for insisting I write this book. It is now written. While I am always encouraging you, your push and tireless efforts help me share with the world these secrets of college classroom success.

Introduction

Dear Prospective and Current College Students,

Congratulations on holding this book in your hands. This is the first step toward opening the doors of endless opportunities for you, both during and after college. You are about to learn what no other college faculty member is willing to tell... the secrets of college classroom success.

I suggest you read every word in this book. Given the competition of social media, I have intentionally made it brief; but pertinent and insightful. After you have read every word, you can then return and simply focus on the helpful tips that can help you maneuver through the classroom environment. My motto is: You should work hard, and play hard, but be smart when doing both.

As I network with faculty members from Harvard, Yale, Miami, Florida State, Florida International University, Michigan State, Boston College, and others, it is clear we all have similar experiences with students. Common scenarios exist amongst faculty members near and far, regardless of age, gender, race, or location. You will learn these secrets known by all faculty members.

You were born to be successful and your journey to success can get off to a great start while you are in college. Think about it, you will take over 40 classes and if each class has at least 40 students and one faculty member, you will have the opportunity to network with at least 1600 students and 40 faculty members. Let's begin to build your collegiate empire.

This book does not cover test-taking tips. I get down to the basics of what it takes to survive in the classroom. I provide ideas that are easy to apply for every student regardless of the

GPA (grade point average). It is not enough to be book-smart; you must have and display character, and exhibit classroom behavior intelligence. So, I encourage you to read and apply. In reading the material in this book, keep in mind that all faculty members are unique. I give general guidelines that may or may not fit your situation specifically. You may need to adjust the advice accordingly.

Cheers to your success,

Prof. Smith

P.S. The helpful tips after each chapter are written in a general sense. You may need to alter the advice given your personality coupled with the faculty member's personality. For example, a helpful tip may state to ask a question. However, before taking action, keep in mind your tone, your body language, and the personality of the faculty member. You may conclude that the helpful tips or the general overall framework of the chapter must be adjusted to accommodate your environment and the individuals involved. You got this! Now go build your empire!

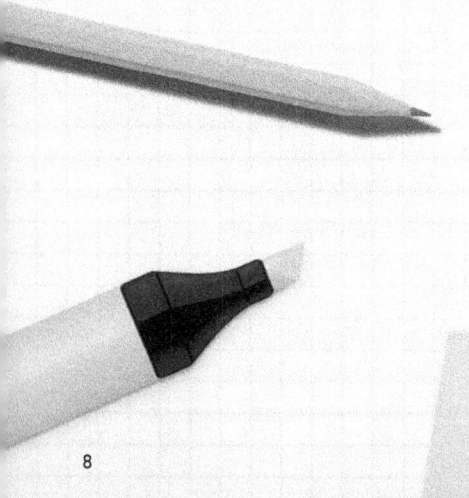

Dear Parent(s):

As parents, we teach our children the principles of character, the importance of an education, and other standards of quality behavior that enhance not only their lives, but mankind. As a college faculty member and a mentor to many undergraduates, graduate students, and alumni from various universities, I have come to realize something very shocking...your child can be unaware of basic "college-life classroom survival skills," or "the art of college-classroom etiquette." Thankfully, I provide those skills here.

Your child is an adult and is protected by privacy laws prohibiting faculty members and university personnel from discussing your child's grades and classroom behavior. After you have done everything you can to prepare them for college, give them the secrets outlined in this book and constantly remind them to reference the material in the book. Then, continue to encourage and support them throughout their college experience.

My insight has been gleaned throughout various classrooms, conversations with students, and faculty members who have shared their classroom experiences. I have also watched the progressive and positive change in students who applied the advice.

After you have done your best to train your college-bound or in-college student in every aspect possible, I promise that the gift of this book will pay off in high returns.

Cheers from one parent to another,

Antoinette

Insider Secrets to College Classroom Success!

Know The Faculty Member

Generally speaking:

When you look at the faculty member, you get an image of a very honorable, respectful individual. However, do not forget that the faculty member is human. Therefore, mistakes will be made; they have feelings, traditions, expectations, historical references, a heart and soul, likes and dislikes.

Seeing the faculty member as a human first and as a faculty member second is not too difficult. He or she was once a student, too. However, now as a faculty member of many students, they are learners for life in their academic area, particularly when it comes to learning the best way to deliver classroom material. Every classroom experience is different for instructors; however, they soar best in a supportive classroom environment. Similarly, when you go to work, regardless of how well you know the material, you will do your best within an environment that brings out the best in you... a place that helps you identify your best aspects and capitalize on them.

In order to be one of the students who bring about positive energy toward the faculty member, you must learn to understand the person teaching; after all, their judgment of you can become a vital key or a thorn to your success. While the faculty member will continue in their career, perhaps never seeing you again, the grade you earn in their class will remain on your transcript. Additionally, several years from now, you may need a letter of recommendation. So the best you can do is view the faculty member from the lens of a human being, like you do your aunt or uncle, your brother or sister, or your friend. When you see someone this way, you approach them differently.

DID YOU KNOW? Every faculty member has a story, good or bad, that shaped them into who they are as an individual. Thus, consider their character and their story.

HELPFUL TIPS: Converse with the instructor during office hours, class breaks, or even in passing. Here are a few questions you can ask one-on-one, not in front of the entire class: Are you from this area? How do you enjoy having the opportunity to impact the lives of so many college students? Outside of teaching and research, what do you enjoy doing? Also, feel free to ask them for career advice.

Laugh at the Faculty Member's "Appropriate" Jokes

My Story:

For years, I have tried to convince my family members that I am a comedian. To prove this statement, I took three of my daughters to class with me one day. Once class was over, I quickly proclaimed to my daughters, "See, I told you I am a comedian." While speaking in agreement, my daughters also suggested that the students only laughed so I would not feel bad. Master's level students can be clever that way…either they laugh because I am funny, because I am corny, or because they feel sorry for me. Whatever the reason, they won. They won by making me feel comfortable. I cannot guess what was in their heads, but my eyes and ears told me that they laughed at my classroom jokes. Thus, we all won.

Generally Speaking:

When a faculty member jokes, he or she is opening up. An exchange of smiles and laughter brings about happiness and creates a positive classroom environment. Your family members and friends are pretty much the only ones you can be truthful with and admit that something was not funny, was corny, or just plain out of left field. However, when it comes to a faculty member who is trying to tell a joke or two, make every effort to at least smile while looking directly at the faculty member, or at your notes, but not other students. Any other move will allow room for negative interpretation.

DID YOU KNOW? Laughing at the faculty member's humor or punch line is a sign that you relate to their understanding of life.

HELPFUL TIPS: When a faculty member laughs, try to laugh with them or at least smile. If you really enjoyed the joke, it is okay to say, "Professor, that was really funny." During the break you could tell the faculty member, "I really enjoy your teaching style. Your humor makes the material interesting and the class exciting."

Understand the Faculty Members' Expectations

Generally Speaking:

Many of you know your parents' expectations. If you are in a relationship, you understand your partner's expectations. You bend over backwards and do what it takes to receive particular outcomes based on those expectations.

My Story:

I recall a semester where I told my students that all Jonathans do well in my class, because my husband's name is Jonathan. It was a joke, of course, but thus far all Jonathans have excelled in my class. During one particular semester with a graduate class, the students began using the word Jonathan as frequently as possible. Their fictitious companies were named things like Jonathan Inc.; their names were modified to include the word Jonathan. There was even a group that used my name and called themselves "Antoinette's Angels." While these students obviously earned their grade, they understood the power of impression management and the halo effect.

My Advice:

Every faculty member and every class is different. Therefore, you must approach each class with an open mind; listening, observing, and watching for clues that will assist you in ascertaining not only the expectations of the syllabus, but those noted by the faculty member. For example, if the faculty member starts class immediately, then an obvious thing to do would be to arrive to class on time. If the faculty member tends to lecture without seeking class participation, then he or she is likely to expect that you take good notes and raise your hand only for clarification, but not to take over the class with a full, drawn-out debate.

DID YOU KNOW? If you know someone's expectations, you began to know what's in his or her mind and heart. Become a winner at mastering expectations.

HELPFUL TIPS: Ask the faculty member to give you an idea of the behavior of students who have passed their class. This will give you insight into what they believe is necessary to succeed in his or her class. You can also ask other students, but asking the professor is also important. Ask what is the best way to study for exams and if the recommended study method is the same for all exams.

Insider Secrets to College Classroom Success!

Establish a Positive Student Profile

Generally Speaking:

Faculty Members rarely sit down with each other to discuss specific students. However, if your name comes up in a conversation amongst those within your major, you want the discussion to be very positive.

My Story:

I recall sitting in my office one day and one of my previous students passed by on his way to see another faculty member. I was disappointed that this student did not speak to me, particularly given that he always spoke. Later that day, the instructor he was visiting came into my office, upset, as she was trying to gather some facts about a cheating incident that took place in her classroom. When she mentioned the name of my previous student, I had nothing but great things to say about him. I am unsure of the outcome, but at least this student, who found himself in an unfortunate situation, left a lasting impression with me that was ultimately shared with another faculty member.

Generally Speaking:

Have you ever heard the saying, "It's a small world"? The scenario above illustrates that point. The world is even smaller in academia. All faculty members, regardless of where they live, particularly within the same major, are likely to either meet face-to-face, or be a phone call or email away. Faculty Members within your department have faculty meetings and certain days of the week that most of them are present in their classroom. They attend alumni and conference events together. The opportunities to network with other faculty members are endless. Because you cannot predict their encounters, or your encounters, it is best to know that you are always on stage when you encounter those charged with teaching in a college setting.

My Advice:

Here are some questions to ask yourself: Do I arrive at class five minutes early? Do I speak to the faculty members? Do I let the faculty member know in advance when, due to serious illness or emergency, I cannot make it to class? Do I apologize after class if I arrive late due to an emergency or unforeseen situation? Do I email the faculty members? What lasting impression do I leave with each of the faculty members? What common view do I want all of the faculty members to have about me?

DID YOU KNOW? You can manage the way the faculty members see you. Yes. Thus, be thankful that the world is small when it comes to faculty members and use it to your advantage.

HELPFUL TIPS: Make compliments about one instructor to another one; that indicates that you connect with their world. Compliment the faculty member on his or her strongest attributes or teaching acumen. Such compliments might sound like, "Hey, Professor, do you know Professor XYZ? I had her in micro-economics. Tell her Benjamin said hi." "Oh, Professor, I really enjoy the way you taught Chapter 3." However, never compliment another faculty member without complimenting the one you are speaking with first. Sometimes just having a conversation that is not directly related to the class helps in making a "normal" connection.

Class interaction is also absolutely vital, whether simply responding to questions or interacting in the form of non-abrasive debates. The point is, find ways to interact in a balanced manner (as you do not want to come across as annoying) with the faculty member during class and during designated office hours.

Make sure the faculty member knows your name by reminding them during one-on-one engagement; whether during breaks, on the telephone, on or off campus. Be sure to pronounce your name and pause between your first and last name. The world has an amazing variety of accents, so be sure your name is heard clearly so that it is remembered clearly.

Additionally, it is essential for you to take part in each classroom experience. Know your classmates and network/interact with other students in the class.

Make Yourself Visible in the Classroom

Generally Speaking:

The letter T is what you should remember when deciding where to sit in college classrooms. I can look back on all of my classes and remember most of the faces of the students who sat in the T-zone. Faculty members seem to notice students in the first two rows and then everyone straight down the middle of the class.

Those students not in the T-zone had to work a little harder to be noticed and leave a lasting impression.

When you sit in the T-zone, however, your main task is to remain attentive and not be a distraction.

The T-zone can also work against you if you are not paying attention or present some form of distraction (e.g., sexy clothing or offensive messages on t-shirts). I recall a student who sat in the T-zone and spent the majority of the class period on the phone and smiling at the messages. They were distracting me from focusing on the material and the other students. I had no choice but to ask the student to put away the phone. If that student had been sitting outside the T-zone, there would not have been such a distraction.

My Story:

I recall having a B+ student in my class who never participated in class discussions. She would, however, visit me in my office and send emails. One day, I was randomly calling on individuals and I called on her. She was not in the T-zone and my immediate thought was that I had never noticed her in the classroom before. Even though she did her impression management behind the scenes, sitting in the T-zone would have been an additional advantage.

My Advice:

If your classroom has an aisle, then the T-zone becomes approximately the first three seats in each row and the seat next to the aisle. For other room setups, such as the U-shape, round tables, auditoriums and more, sit in the middle or on the side that your faculty member seems to favor the most. For example, if your faculty member has a habit of standing or looking to the left, then find a seat in that general area.

DID YOU KNOW? Every decision counts, including where you sit and how you interact.

HELPFUL TIPS: If you can be attentive during class, arrive early and claim your T-zone seat until your classmates recognize that the seat belongs to you. If you cannot remain attentive, then do not sit in the back but sit to the far right or the far left and in any row except the first, second, or last two rows. Thus, you do not appear to purposely be avoiding the faculty member. If you are attentive and the T-zone is not available, increase your level of participation.

Kill the Smirk - No "Smirk Students" Allowed

Generally speaking:

Every faculty member - at least once during their career - encounters the smirk student. The smirk student is not a common one, but is worthy of discussion. Could you be that smirk student?

If you do not know the "smirk student," let me introduce them. Can you imagine yourself preparing for a big day at work? The excitement and anticipation builds. You run through all of your preparation mentally, time and time again. Then, the moment arrives and you are standing in front of 45-plus individuals and you are ready to speak. You begin to deliver the material and share information with the audience. During one of your proudest moments, while speaking your eyes scan the room and you quickly identify the "smirk student"! Yes, you notice a smirk on someone's face. No one else has this smirk, but this person looks directly at you, with a facial expression that reads, "What you're telling me is a bunch of crap! C-R-A-P! Crap!"

Every faculty member is aware of the "smirk student". Do not be that student! Do not be the one that wears that condescending smile or sarcastic twinkle; nor the one with any body language that can be read as, "I could not care less about what you are saying" or "you are speaking a bunch of bull." The smirk look that reads, "I do not believe nor respect what you are saying" may potentially ruin any future encounter you have with this faculty member and others.

My Story:

I recall a student I absolutely adored; and I found myself speaking of this student to another faculty member. The faculty member responded, "He has this smirk on his face during class that absolutely annoys me." I explained how the student never showed a smirk in my class. One day, this same student attended a workshop and there his smirk appeared, loud and clear. While the 30 other participants were attentive, I could only focus on the smirk. After the workshop, I told the student that his smirk made me quite uncomfortable. It turns out that he was unaware of his facial expression…hmmm, the same facial expression that left a bad impression with my colleague.

My Advice:

If you are unsure of what look to portray during a presentation, the safe expression is a positive, eager-to-learn one. If you have doubts or a varying opinion, maintaining a tactful posture is best; and raising a polite question may be warranted. The smirk, however, sends a discouragingly loud message that is likely to reflect negatively on your character. The smirk I am referring to is not your typical smile or a laugh, but it comes with a conceited or offensive attitude.

Did you know? When you are not speaking, your body language speaks for you. Therefore, pay attention to your body language, and be conscious of what it is saying to the one paying attention to you.

Helpful Tips: Avoid side conversations and laughing that interrupts the faculty member and disrupts the flow of education. Find ways to communicate with each faculty member, even if you just simply say hello. If you are the smirk student, there are ways to help the faculty member understand that you are not being disrespectful. Sit and listen intentionally. Nod your head at times to indicate that you are listening. Raise your hand with a question or statement a minimum of four times throughout the course. For example, "Professor, I recall in Chapter 1 when you gave us the example of XYZ. Is the material in this chapter an extension of the material we learned in Chapter 1?" Such a question signals that you were listening previously and you continue to listen intently. Be aware of your facial expressions as you are listening to the faculty members. Avoid bored expressions and attempt to keep a happy (or in the very least – interested) expression on your face. Tell yourself that you want to be there, even when you do not - it shows on your face and in your body language. Make sure you get enough sleep at home to avoid sleeping during class.

Contacting The Faculty Member Before and After Class - What a Brilliant Idea!

My Advice:

There are students the faculty member has heard about, will meet on the first day of class, or will have met prior to class. You want to be the student the faculty member meets prior to class - under your terms. The best approach is likely contacting the faculty member by email instead of face-to-face. Prior to your class's start date, the faculty member is likely involved in research activity, working with students they currently have in their course, preparing for your class, or returning from a break. Sending an email to introduce yourself and request the syllabus indicates that you are preparing for the class. Most students will not request the syllabus beforehand, so do yourself a favor and begin with a great impression before your classmates do. Additionally, if you reach out to your faculty member several years after graduating, they will have the ability to search your name in their email and recall that you were preparing yourself for class, and there are many other benefits to being proactive in communicating.

My Story:

Before the beginning of the spring semester, approximately five days before class, Mohammed requested the course syllabus. His email stated, "Hi Professor, My name is Mohammed and I am in your ACG XXXX course on Tuesday mornings. I look forward to meeting you and taking your course. Could you kindly send me a copy of your syllabus so that I may properly be prepared on the first day?" This was perfect and timely. Monica, on the other hand, sent an email during the fall semester requesting the syllabus for the upcoming summer semester. The email request was written nicely but the timing was awful. While Mohammed requested the syllabus within a reasonable amount of time, when I would have the syllabus done and readily available, Monica requested the summer syllabus in December, approximately six months beforehand. I explained to Monica that the syllabus was not ready and she followed up by requesting the current syllabus. While this may be a normal request for Monica's other faculty members, to me it felt like pressure. A syllabus is a tool that the faculty member uses to communicate objectives with current students and the syllabus is subject to change throughout the year and for each class. So I wrote another, more detailed, message to Monica explaining that I was in the middle of preparing for final exams, that the current syllabus is only for current students, and my summer syllabus is completely different from my fall syllabus. That was the last I heard from Monica.

My Advice:

Start working on the class at least one week prior to the very first day by getting the syllabus a few days early and browsing the required course material. Do not wait until finals' week or even after the final to ask for extra credit. In other words, work on your grade from the very beginning. The overall goal is to be prepared from the very first day, and stay prepared.

Then there are students who send an email to the faculty member simply thanking them for a great semester. If you feel as if the teacher added value to your life, or helped you learn something that you did not clearly understand prior to the class, never hesitate to share the compliment, even if you disliked the faculty member. Keep in mind that you can always find kind words for everyone, so find kind words to send to the faculty member and send them immediately after you have taken your final exam or right after final grades are posted.

DID YOU KNOW? 1 cup of timeliness, 1 teaspoon of brevity, 1 gallon of addressing the faculty member appropriately (e.g., Hi, Professor Smith), 0 ounces of slang (e.g., What's Up or LOL), and 2 tablespoons of humility are the typical ingredients of well written communication to the faculty member.

HELPFUL TIPS: Send an email requesting the syllabus three to five days before the class start date, but never within one to two days or a month or more in advance. Briefly introduce yourself within the email, using one or two sentences. Send an email up to three days after your final exam, finding one or two things for which to thank the faculty member.

After addressing the faculty member as either Professor or Dr. (regardless of their title, or even if they have given you permission to call them by their first name), your next sentence could be something similar to: "I hope all is well," "I hope you enjoyed your summer," "How are you?" "I've heard wonderful things about you."

Asking the Faculty Member to Bend the Rules for You – Hmmm

Generally Speaking:

The saying goes, "never say never," and there are some situations where it is appropriate for the faculty member to bend the rules (e.g., death, serious injury or illness, military and religious requirements, and personal/business matters). There are students who experience major problems such as unexpected family or personal problems. In such cases, you want to notify the faculty member immediately and if you have to provide short notice - explain that as well. Thus, "never" is somewhat extreme, but the goal is to move cautiously and humbly, keeping in mind that the faculty member may independently verify your information.

Faculty members have encountered or heard every possible cause of emotional stress from a student. The most popular categories are the cries: "I'll lose my scholarship", "I'll lose my financial aid", "I'm an A student and I do not understand what went wrong", "I'm taking so many classes", "My job is so time-consuming", or students will simply challenge a test. If you believe a faculty member graded a question incorrectly, simply approach the problem in a way that points to you: "Professor, I am very confused because I thought the answer was C. Do you mind explaining this problem to me so that I can get it correct in the future?" As you watch the faculty member, the error will become obvious to either you or the faculty member. The best approach is to take responsibility and then ask for advice.

My Advice:

Go to the faculty member, but you must take full responsibility. By filling the faculty member in on the details of your life, you are asking them to consider how your personal situation impacted your performance. They are likely aware of other students who have been in similar or worse situations, but still excelled in their classes. Additionally, after grading, the faculty member will know of specific questions that were challenging or problematic for most students.

DID YOU KNOW? With the right approach, the right circumstances, and simply doing your best, advantages are likely to come your way when you least expect it.

HELPFUL TIPS: Always inform the faculty member of your class-related concerns prior to meeting with the faculty member. If your concerns relate to specific questions, identify the questions beforehand. If your concerns are not as specific, give the faculty member the subject of your requested meeting so he or she can be prepared. For example, "Professor, I have some concerns about my performance in class. I would like to meet with you in order to figure out how I can do better. I cannot meet during your office hours, but is there a time I can reach you by phone or other means?" This way, the faculty member can prepare for your visit. The more prepared your faculty member is, the better the outcome will be.

#3 Learn to Make Tough Decisions

Disagree, With Dignity and Humility (and Hold the Attitude)

My Advice:

There may be times when you will have a disagreement with the faculty member. When you have a concern, do not address the classroom; address the faculty member by raising your hand. Do not compare your grade to another student's grade. Simply go to the faculty member and speak about your specific grade without bringing others into the issue. Perhaps you computed your final grade to be higher than the faculty member's calculation or you disagree with the grading of a problem. Never challenge the faculty member in front of the class. Simply go to them during break, or visit them during office hours or by requesting an appointment. The goal is to disagree without being rude. The idea of learning is that it is okay to disagree. A healthy disagreement can be an enjoyable learning experience for both you and the faculty member.

My Story:

Every student should clearly understand how to compute their grade and ask for clarification on any grading concerns. I recall a student who failed an essay and was given an F. He left me a voicemail message and sent several emails demanding to speak with me and, in so many words, threatened to report me to the Department Chair and the Dean. When the student arrived at my office, he immediately sat down and stated, "Professor, my work was excellent and you gave me an F." He then backed up his statement with his work experience and other grades he'd earned in previous classes. Never once did he humble himself and ask where he went wrong. Never once did he ask if I would explain what I needed in the essays. Never once did he ask how to improve his grade. He simply acted like he was doing me a favor by being in my classroom. He immediately became humble and apologetic once I showed him the A+ work of his classmates (of course with names deleted) and how his responses were sub-par.

DID YOU KNOW? It is not what you say, but how you say it. Tone and attitude is everything.

HELPFUL TIPS: Schedule office time with the faculty member to discuss all grade-related issues, and try to contact the faculty member within 24 hours of receiving your grade or feedback. Make your request to the faculty member using a humble and simple approach. Ask for clarification as to how to achieve your end result. Never threaten to go to the Dean or above the faculty member. Academic grade appeal processes typically start with the faculty member, so going above typically can't be done until the student meets with the faculty member. If you must go beyond the faculty member, keep a humble tone and state, "Professor, I thank you for your time in trying to help me understand. However, I do not agree. Do you mind if I elevate the matter, just to ensure all appropriate measures were taken?" Wait for the faculty member's response and proceed in a similar manner, humble and forward, if necessary.

Dealing With A Faculty Member Whose Behavior Causes Discomfort

Generally Speaking:

In every aspect of life and business, there is the good, the bad, and the ugly. The academia environment is no different. Thus, as a student, in addition to understanding how to achieve success in the classroom (the good), you should also be aware that incidents sometimes occur that can make it difficult for you to achieve success (the bad). In rare cases (the ugly), this may be due to the faculty member's behavior. As faculty members, what we say and how we conduct ourselves is important to setting the overall tone of the classroom. A faculty member at any rank can engage in misconduct.

Throughout your academic experience, you are likely to experience one of the following: (a) A faculty member's off-color statements or jokes; (b) a course that becomes a waste of your time and money given the faculty member's excessive (the word excessive is emphasized here) discussions of non-course topics (e.g., personal matters); or (c) being unfairly treated (i.e., harassment or discrimination). If you have any of these classroom experiences, the worst thing you can do is be quiet, as eliminating such behavior is of great importance to any university.

My Advice:

Before I go any further, however, I want to cover some ground rules.

The first rule is, within your first year of college come up with a list of potential mentors, some who work on campus and non-campus individuals who have a successful career. Listen closely to those you meet; and ask yourself if they have a passion for people. Also, determine if they think, logically, from a higher perspective. And, ask yourself can you trust them. You are likely to find campus individuals in positions such as clerical, advising, faculty members, and career services. You will need a mentor to assist you through difficult college experiences.

The second rule is to ask yourself if the issue is more the result of a personality difference, cultural difference, or some other aspect unrelated to what the university would consider interfering with its student mission. Consider listening to your "inner voice" or posing a general scenario to your mentor or a close friend in order to get a neutral perspective. Ask yourself the following questions: Have I noticed other adverse reactions from fellow students? Have their been similar complaints? Did I voice my concern to the professor? Do not talk with friends who are troublemakers, instead seek out wise counsel and talk to your parents.

Once you have covered these ground rules, when you encounter such difficult situations where the faculty member is the source of your discomfort, you have an option to do nothing, go directly to the faculty member either anonymously or non-anonymously, go to the director/chair of the department, report the issue to the university; and then, in very rare and extreme cases, go directly to the dean of the college. In all instances, find your university's policy and follow the indicated procedure.

Rarely will a case justify going directly to the dean or the university. In an academic environment, a faculty member oversees the classroom, the director oversees the department, the dean oversees the college, and the president oversees the university. Thus, with any complaint, you are encouraged to follow this hierarchical structure by first starting with the source, if that is so directed in the policy.

If it is a situation in which you feel comfortable speaking with the faculty member either anonymously or non-anonymously, then do so as it gives the faculty member an opportunity to understand your perspective and respond accordingly.

In the event you are uncomfortable going directly to the faculty member or the problem was unresolved with the faculty member (such as incidents of harassment or discrimination), then you are free to go to the department chair either anonymously or non-anonymously. Give the department chair an opportunity to address your concerns, while keeping your mentor in the loop of all conversations for guidance. Again, follow the university's policy, typically posted at the university's web page.

If you feel that your problem remains unresolved, then your next course of action (even prior to going to the Dean) is to file a complaint through the university system (e.g., student complaints and appeals office).

Of all the helpful advice that I have outlined in this book, the advice in this chapter is by far the most general and heartfelt. In the beginning of this chapter, I mentioned the worst thing you can do is be quiet. Not keeping quiet, comes in the form of thinking about the situation, and deciding if and how you will move forward, if necessary. If you have thought through the process and decided to not move forward, then you have listened to your voice and the perhaps the voice of mentor and others. If your decision is to move forward, then think every step through and be open to the advice of these others, particularly the feedback from the department chair.

DID YOU KNOW? Your emotions cloud your judgment. Thus, never complain when you are upset. Instead wait until at least the next day and reassess your feelings.

HELPFUL TIPS: Remember to get a mentor within your first year. Always keep your mentor in the loop, from your initial to your last communication, including the feedback and responses received along your journey. Whenever legally possible, document the incident. Do not delete any emails, or other supporting documentation. It may be a legal violation, however, to tape a faculty member without the faculty member's consent.

Do You Feel like Somebody's Watching You? They Are

Generally Speaking:

Yes, they are. Your classmates are watching you, and who knows, they may one day become your competition, your boss, or your subordinate. Your fellow students, particularly the cream of the crop, will remember you for good or for bad. You must remember that the world is indeed small and social media makes it seem even smaller, allowing us to leave impressions on others who are not in the same location. You never know who is watching you. When you are not impressive to the faculty member, you are likely unimpressive to your classmates. They may never share their opinion of you unless circumstances warrant it.

My Story:

I recall a lunch hour where several of the faculty members were meeting with executives from a large and prominent firm. The executives were on campus recruiting current students and alumni, and some of those from the firm were alumni of the university. One alumnus told a story of an interview that took place the day before. She spoke of a former classmate, who was seeking a job at her firm. She described her facial expression as the classmate approached the firm's booth. The classmate had done everything correctly and her resume was very impressive. However, one thing went wrong. A partner of the firm noticed the associate's facial expression as the woman approached. She had no other choice but to describe how she remembered her classmate's behavior some years ago, and how it left her with a bad impression regarding her work ethic and personality. Needless to say, the classmate was not called for a second interview.

DID YOU KNOW? The college classroom is like a movie scene…you are the star and your actions are recorded and remain in the faculty member's mental archives far beyond the immediate classroom setting.

HELPFUL TIPS: Speak to other classmates. Work as a leader or a supporter when it comes to group projects. Never talk badly about another student, even to the faculty member. If the faculty member asks for your opinion about another student, keep your response short and try to simply say, "Professor, I just do my best to make sure I do things correctly." Never speak badly about a faculty member to another faculty member or to another student. These suggestions are your most cautious stance. You want to be the one who works hard on the team project and not the one who needs to be carried. You want to be the one willing to take the lead on discussions and, in fact, the lead on the team.

Disassociate Yourself from Disruptive Students

This is not a student who is engaged and someone the faculty member enjoys. However, this is a student who is clearly disruptive and obviously changes the mood of the faculty member and the class in a disruptive way. The disruptive student comes in several forms that potentially disrupt classroom time. In the classroom, faculty members experience students completing their assignments from other classes, consistently arriving late or leaving early, talking excessively, surfing the Internet, text messaging, sleeping, aggressively challenging the faculty member's position, and doing everything except enjoying the classroom for the purpose of learning.

In class, you will pick your favorite seat and it will feel comfortable to you. However, if you select a seat next to the person who is constantly challenging the faculty member or disrupting the class in any way, do your best to move over a seat or two, even an entire row (if possible). Perhaps the faculty member will make the assumption that you are friends. You have to manage your image, because whom you associate with could impact your grade in the class, and employment – remember those letters of recommendation. When this person leaves the classroom during breaks, sit in your seat a little longer or move a little quicker to clearly signal that you do not support their behavior.

DID YOU KNOW? Birds of a feather flock together, so flock with classroom birds that respect the classroom etiquette; or be your own respectful bird.

HELPFUL TIPS: Draw a clear line between you and the source of the disruption. There is always a price to pay. If you have no choice but to sit next to a disruptive student, look down or away during any moments he or she is clearly disrupting the class. Do your best not to support disruptive behavior by laughing, smiling, looking, or validating the behavior in any way.

Remember to turn off, or at least silence, all non-essential electronic devices, and use them only to look at class materials. Do not use class time for emailing, texting, and social media, unless such use is authorized by the faculty member.

The Art of Treating Your Professor Like an Academic Ferrari

Generally Speaking:

A Ferrari is a luxury vehicle that serves many purposes for many people, from being a showpiece to a racing vehicle. The word 'Ferrari' creates powerful images, and gets immediate respect. Some faculty members have a Ph.D. and some do not. Once a faculty member obtains their Ph.D., they have their Doctorate of Philosophy. When in doubt, refer to each faculty member, as Dr. or Professor and never Mr. or Mrs. You can always ask, "How should I address you?" The goal is to assume they have the highest title unless you determine otherwise.

My Story:

Such insight can be useful throughout life. For example, I recall walking into a facility and running into a man who was sweeping the floor. I was about to deliver a speech and I needed to set up. Before asking him for directions or anything else, my first question was, "Excuse me, sir, are you the supervisor?" Oh, wow, did his eyes light up and his posture became stronger and more upright. He smiled when he responded, "Oh, no, I am not the supervisor; but how can I help you?" As a result of the upgraded title I had given this gentleman, he was encouraged even more to help me with everything I needed. From that moment forward, I did not have to lift a finger. He made sure everything was spectacular…the most sparkling water glass I had ever seen was provided. He adjusted the lighting and the temperature in the room, and he made sure that I had more than enough copies of my handouts. This is the impact you want to have on the faculty member. Titles are important to many people. You do not want to make the mistake of "under-titling" someone.

DID YOU KNOW? Everyone loves an automatic boost in ego, earned or unearned. A little upgrade leaves a BIG impression.

HELPFUL TIPS: Learn about the faculty member, find out their appropriate title, and use it.

If you do not know the ranking of the faculty member (e.g., lecturer, instructor, or faculty member), refer to them as faculty member and not Mr., Mrs., or Ms.

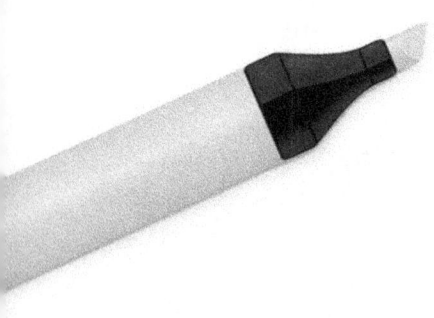

Be A Team Player

Encouraging the Faculty Member

Generally Speaking:

Whether it is sports, a speech, preparing for a big day, a recital, or taking a test, every human being likes to be encouraged. Every class meeting is that big moment for the faculty member. Each class period for the faculty member could range from a complete disaster to a class that wins the "GREATEST FACULTY MEMBER OF ALL TIMES" award. One bad move or one wrong word could end a faculty member's career, particularly if he or she is untenured. Think about the challenge, particularly for new instructors, of being responsible for connecting with 30-plus students in the classroom.

My Advice:

I recall a student who stated, "Professor, I really disliked this assignment, but I appreciate the assignment so much. I have never been forced to look at the material in such detail, but I got so much from the material." This conversation reassured me that I was giving the students something of value. Another student stated, "Professor, I really like how you give us these random assignments to solve during class."

Encourage the faculty member with words or a thumbs-up and try to do so particularly after a difficult class or even if the faculty member is seasoned and always does an outstanding job.

DID YOU KNOW? Everyone likes to hear good things about themselves.

HELPFUL TIPS: If you genuinely enjoyed something in the class, please feel free to tell the faculty member and share the details. Encourage the faculty member with a smile. Encourage the faculty member by looking directly at him or her when he or she is speaking. During the break or after class, say a kind word to the faculty member such as, "I like your teaching style," "For such a difficult topic, you do well in helping us learn," or "If I become a faculty member, I am going to use some of your teaching techniques." Avoid giving the faculty member advice, simply offer encouragement in areas where the faculty member does well.

These are goods tips in all aspects of life. Just as you as students like to be encouraged, we like to be encouraged. It helps to be an encourager in all aspects of life, from encouraging one's health care professional, one's co-worker, one's boss, etc. Stop after class and tell another student that they answered a question particularly well, or asked a question you hadn't thought of.

Success is a WE Thing!

Generally Speaking:

Faculty members are in the business of helping others succeed. Therefore, when you help other students, the faculty member is likely to identify with you as a person. Additionally, you are demonstrating that you have learned from them in a way that allows you to proficiently share with others.

My Story:

I recall encouraging students to post their questions for me on the discussion board, regarding homework and other material. I also encouraged them to respond if they could help fellow students. Jennifer and Omar would do just that, helping classmates out with both minor and major details. Interestingly enough, neither Jennifer nor Omar volunteered during class discussions. However, through their willingness to help, I was eager to figure out who they were. They left a lasting impression on me without volunteering during class hours. Additionally, during lab hours it was difficult for me to get to every student who fell behind. Some students chose to remain seated, tend to their cell phones, or enjoy conversations with others as they waited for the few to catch up. However, those who decided to make a move to help out left a powerful, lasting impression. Remember, your time is precious. Only help out if you have time to do so. Otherwise, remove helping other students from your to-do-list.

DID YOU KNOW? The generosity in you is free, and goes a long way.

HELPFUL TIPS: Respond to students who post questions on classroom forums, such as discussion boards. When a faculty member is having a hard time getting to a student, or answering a student's question, ask the faculty member if you can attempt to help them. You may be able to help a fellow student who is in need of extra instruction.

Insider Secrets to College Classroom Success!

Prepare for the Unexpected

Computing Your Course Grade

Generally Speaking:

It amazes me when students sit back and do not understand the grading system outlined in the syllabus or how to compute their grade. Not understanding is okay, but the not asking is the part that amazes me. If you do not understand how to compute your grade, or how to keep up your grade in the course, you should ask the faculty member to explain the grading criteria, rubric, and weighting again until you understand. This is the most important factor in achieving your best grade and setting your expectations.

My Story:

A former student appeared not to understand how to compute their grade. The midterm was worth major points toward the overall course grade. However, there was another assignment on the syllabus that was worth very minimal points. As a matter of fact, a student could get an F on this assignment and still obtain an A. Johnny came to see me, extremely concerned about getting an A on the minimal assignment. I helped Johnny with the assignment, but asked him if he had time to focus on the midterm. Johnny replied, "I will, but not until I get this assignment done." With the midterm only two days away, I wondered if Johnny truly understood the weight of the midterm versus the weight of the minimal point assignment. Even after I hinted to Johnny about the points' proportion, he was determined to spend the majority of my office hours discussing the assignment and asked nothing about the midterm. I became so frustrated that I no longer hinted, but definitively pointed out his error in thinking and computed the numbers for him one day before the midterm. Johnny's midterm grade and final class grade reflected his lack of understanding about the grading system on the syllabus.

DID YOU KNOW? Not all grades are treated equally, so spend the most time on the assignments that carry the most weight.

HELPFUL TIPS: On the first day of class or as soon as possible, ask the faculty member to explain how he or she computes grades, even if you feel as though you understand. Enter hypothetical grades and then have the faculty member verify your understanding. If you use a system that computes your grades, ask the faculty member how accurate the system is compared to their calculation.

Prepare for What You Can't Prepare for

Generally Speaking:

Throughout your college experience, you are likely to have a pop quiz, to have questions on a test that were never covered in class, or to be called on by the faculty member to answer a question. As a college student, you must prepare for such events. There are various wise responses that have been used by students when I have unexpectedly called on them in class.

My Story:

I recall Gene who looked at me with such fear. He appeared so frightened that he could not utter a word, as hands from other students were raised excitedly to help. Obviously, Gene had not read the chapter and was not paying attention. This is the reason I called on him. Gene sent me an email apologizing. "Professor, I feel bad that I couldn't answer your question today. I promise I will do better." Gene raised his hand to participate during subsequent classes. Olivia took a different approach when she did not know the answer. She called on her friend to answer the question, which made the entire class and me laugh. Olivia showed that she was quick on her feet. Then there was Scott, who responded, "Professor, that is a great question but I don't know the answer." Scott complimented the faculty member (me) and immediately admitted that he did not have an answer. Scott came across as honest, respectful, humble, and intelligent. I knew Scott was attentive in class, and this was one time he honestly did not know the answer.

While I give quizzes, my quizzes are rare and students are told in advance or given some warning beforehand. Catherine, however, was obviously used to pop quizzes during her college life. She would work on end-of-chapter material and visit me during my office hours for the answers. When she did not visit me, she would send emails asking me to check the accuracy of her work. Catherine made it clear that she was taking five classes and working part-time, and her goal was to stay ahead. She would always ask me if the material she was studying would be on a quiz or test and she made it clear that she wanted to avoid any surprises. Having to work closely with

Catherine provided feedback for me on the teaching material. It also held me accountable for not quizzing the class on anything that Catherine was not particularly prepared for. Catherine did an excellent job in minimizing her risk in the pop quiz area.

My Advice:

When you are aware of a test, such as the midterm and the final exam, always visit your faculty member during their office hours at least a week before the test. During this time, have the faculty member explain the material that you are struggling with. Stephanie always visited my office with a notepad full of questions and referenced page numbers. She would have either a simple question about a concept or need a full lecture. I found myself communicating with Stephanie in a way that guided her focus. I would say things like, "do not worry about that" or "let me explain this, because need you to master this material." So, Stephanie's visits allowed her to get additional insight as to what to study for the exam beyond what was announced to the entire class.

DID YOU KNOW? You can best prepare to take tests by reviewing course material on a daily basis and listening closely to which topics the faculty member emphasizes.

HELPFUL TIPS: When life is too busy, take 15 minutes a day, a few hours before class to read at least one concept from the textbook or other material that will be covered during class. Thus, you have a basis for asking at least one question or making a statement that is supported by the class material. Also, attempt one or two course exercises (e.g., pick a textbook problem, a problem from a handout or online, etc.) a week and email the problem to the faculty member for feedback. If the faculty member does not assign homework, find an article that may relate to the class or be of interest to the faculty member and try to email or mention an article to the faculty member at least once a semester.

You Do Know There is Class Today - Right?

Generally Speaking:

Throughout your college experience, you will find classes you enjoy attending and those you do not enjoy as much. Regardless of how you feel about the course or the faculty member, make an effort to go to each class. By going to class, you will learn the material from the faculty member's perspective and, if you listen closely, the material covered during class will help guide your focus on the material and give valuable clues when it's time to study for exams.

It is also important that the faculty member is familiar with you and your class attendance. For example, do you have a relative or a friend who very seldom came around? Because of their frequent absence, you never made a quality connection with them during the times that they were around. You know each other's names and how you are related, but that is the extent of it. Now, let's suppose this same distant relative asks to borrow $100 because they lost their job. How would you feel about lending $100 to a relative you barely see and have little or no connection with?

In the context of the classroom, a similar situation can occur between a faculty member and a student. There are students who will never miss a day of class and will email the faculty member in advance if an emergency arises. These same students will tell the faculty member when they are arriving late or leaving early. On the other hand, there are students who have a habit of missing the first day of class for every class. There are other students who come the first day and on exam days. Finally, there are students who come to class around their work or social schedule.

My Advice:

The purpose of going to class is not just to learn the material, but to observe the faculty member. During class, notice how excited the faculty member gets when teaching specific concepts. Additionally, pay attention to how long he or she spends on certain material.

DID YOU KNOW? Every faculty member favors students who are interested in their material.

HELPFUL TIPS: On the first day of class, exchange contact information with at least three students so that you can contact them whenever you miss class. Ensure that at least one of your contacts sits in the first two rows on your first day. Whenever you are absent, do not contact the faculty member to ask what was covered. Instead, contact a student for the material and then later confirm with the faculty member what material was covered.

We All Know the Dog Doesn't Eat Your Homework

Generally Speaking:

Faculty members put a lot of thought into your homework assignments. Homework is not to torture students, but for practice, out-of-classroom experience and exposure, and learning through research. Faculty members give homework as a way of assisting you in learning the material, enforcing concepts, and earning points. Homework is one of the easiest ways to earn points, as you have all the resources available to you outside of the classroom. Homework also signals what will be on your upcoming exam. Whether your homework is being graded and collected is unimportant, as the homework assignments assist you in achieving a desired outcome.

DID YOU KNOW? A little more effort goes a long way. The payoff does not have to be immediate in order to have the biggest bang.

HELPFUL TIPS: If some of the homework problems are too difficult, still do your best to complete the assignment. Submit your homework prior to the due date, and ask the faculty member to provide feedback. The other option is to visit the faculty member for feedback.

Always do your best to answer the questions thoroughly, particularly the first three questions. The first set of questions will help you achieve the halo effect in grading, where the faculty member is likely to judge that you have done a great job for the entire homework assignment. Turn in your homework on time. Here is another little secret - some faculty develop quizzes and test questions from the homework.

Insider Secrets to College Classroom Success!

Bonus Advice

Beyond the Classroom

College life provides an opportunity for higher learning in every category of your life. While your coursework is of highest priority, attempt to leave some energy to branch out beyond the classroom, as you must grow overall as a person.

Your school is likely to have strong ties with the community and leaders from the community will interact with the students in ways such as serving as a speaker, lecturer, or offering community service opportunities. It is important that you attend such events, as doing so will give you the opportunity to grow and network.

Joining and becoming an officer in extracurricular groups and clubs will put you ahead of the pack when it comes to networking and job opportunities. Look on your school's website for sorority and fraternity opportunities. These organizations are involved in leadership, awarding scholarships, service, athletics, social events, and more.

I once asked a student how did she land a job with one of the leading social media companies in Atlanta, GA and she replied, "I am a self starter. I took the lead in inviting and organizing various companies to visit our university. While my university was doing similar events, I felt the need to focus speaking on social media companies and thus here I am." I tell you this story to demonstrate that as a student, at times, you will have to step outside the box, use your unique gifts, and brand yourself as a leader. You can do it! Just do it! Perhaps you were sent to the school to lead in untapped areas.

One principle you should embrace as a fundamental fact is that you will need to grow, transitioning from various stages in your life. You will need to grow in wisdom (e.g., intellectually, cognitively) and the company you keep, as it will impact how you acquire and assess information and opportunities. On campus, mentors are all around to help you will everything from scholarships, developing or connecting with leadership, dealing with difficult situations and celebrating your achievements. A mentor will give you a better chance at being successful. Also, I suggest you have several mentors or all ages, races, and backgrounds.

HELPFUL TIPS: Do your research…Visit your school's website and search for university and college-level scholarships. The Internet is also great for determining which fraternities and sororities are involved in community activities and landing jobs with major companies that grab your attention or fit your passion.

Additionally, search the Internet using the word mentor and the name of your school to see which faculty members have served as mentors. Seek mentors in your desired field and mentors who can fine-tune your weak areas. When it comes to your mentor, give him or her permission to be honest with their input. Make finding a mentor a priority in your life. A mentor can highlight characteristics that can hinder your growth. When your mentor gives you guidance or an assignment, do not just hear the information, but be a "doer" of what your mentor has discussed with you.

www.ingramcontent.com/pod-product-compliance
Lightning Source LLC
Chambersburg PA
CBHW031217090426
42736CB00009B/949